And
Sandpipers
She
Said

Books by Donald Junkins

The Sunfish and the Partridge
The Graves of Scotland Parish
Walden, 100 Years After Thoreau
And Sandpipers She Said

And
Sandpipers
She
Said

Donald Junkins

The University of Massachusetts Press

Amherst 1970

Some of the poems in this book
have appeared in
The Antioch Review
The Massachusetts Review
Midwest Quarterly
East Coast Poets
Providence Sunday Journal
Quabbin
United Church Herald
The Far Point
The Minnesota Review
The Northwest Review.

For Mardie,
Karn, Daniel & Theodore

Contents

And

Sandpipers

She

Said

Popponesset Beach,
August 1967
_____

and sandpipers you
said walking
from the beach changing
the subject the scrub pines
cooling still
toward our rented
cottage
          where he came
that afternoon gobbling
pills to your soft no
reciting letters wobbling
on the hot sand your
brother easing
him toward the Mustang

they see everything you
said touching
my arm I've never
seen them running

as scared as they ran
today
  on the beach
  your mother said men
  scare me
on the dead
run water cocks
    legging it
the surf seething
at their feet

he just fell all apart you
said changing
the subject again touching
my arm I've never seen
that before
    the children
trailing golden
beach towels

behind us water
Scots bleached
            jack daws

coddered
bag pipers their bellies
salt on our mouths
                later
as we kissed

Your Coming

moving as you
do those things
around the room
moving as you

touch the children
breathing in their
rooms of things
alive geraniums

in an iron pot coming
to life cedar
trees outside
the window moving

as you make our
life a Kirman
rug chrysanthemums
moving yellow

rust the past now
grape juices our mouths
our hands clusters
on antique chairs

moving as you
touch the moist earth
iris crocus tulip
bulbs a house

our yard woods
moving yes
yes now
your breasts

yes trees rooms
stop everything
moving as you
do

October
Cranberry Picking,
Great East Lake
_____

back
in the autumn
boat moving
by the shore
the three horse
power motor
easing my uncle
harry teeth in
the wind piloting
by the islands

we move
the deep
boulders out
of sight toward
land you smile
nod to the river
becalmed
now with oars

pushing the grass
parting

wait
here we asked
the boys nodding
we sloshed to dry
land under the berries
hard bombling our galvanized
buckets disappear beneath
the grass slicing
our hands bending over
the boys yelling

daddy I stand
up you stand
up uncle harry
stands the boys
grin waving red

mittens down
we go again
handfuls
of berries in the dry
grass coming

for years
uncle harry said
only stevens knows
they're here moving
toward the boat
picking eleven
quarts in twenty
minutes our buckets
full the boys' shoes
off the motor

down in the mud
oars floating still
beside the boat we

pushed off again
the wind blowing
the end of
a season
and sky the shore
line now only
sounds of the motor

the smell of wood smoke
you
and the feeling
of the year

Seminary, First Autumn

my old groin pull
nagging the blonde
librarian *Life* size
cover girl (I checked
the stacks) typing
at my left
      megaphones
bleating
from the Charles

those afternoons
those times
lost tapping
keys
    crotchety
those coxwains last
down below the goldfish
goggling the river jelly
fish those old
safes drifting

up in that library
room we were
Brightman's boys
our balls burning
             she's not like
             the rest, the female head
             librarian confided
with Walter Rauschenbusch
and the social
             gospel
she's not, no
hell no

shells traced
the river
             crewel
in our hands
this work
scholarship those
sunny afternoons those

book cards blurring
the day black Phil
Cousins burst
that upstairs back
room with ''the supreme court
desegregated
the schools!''
             we thought

we knew
desiring we thought
we knew how
far away
from books it all
was
             down there aching
             over the long
             pull
fine blonde

hairs those
lost years

jacking
          nightmare deer
          rooms turning
off the mind
classifying Barth
and Brunner
day and night
falling
          all over
ourselves

From the Reservoir
　—for Kitty—

letting your hair
down little by
little standing waist
deep the lake at midnight
calm your head
down reaching
over the water

between us a hand
from your hair
my pocket
　　　　bulging
the hills loomed
over us the rain
at first soft

a flashlight flickering
in the grove the cops
we thought later
we knew it

wasn't the pine there
                when
the grove the sky the light

turned the rain
smashed the lake huddled
over our backs
yes and quiet
dark the trees in their own
image over us walking
           toward the car

To the Coast,
December 1966
_____

flying out of
boston
         tourist
classes over
borders down
there behind
it all
         where will you
         stay you wrote
         not here
at thirty-five
thousand
exactly and
inexactness
everywhere

the sun going
down there
ahead

        all promises
        undefined
        now

stereophonic
multiplying
sunsets
and my second
gin and tonic
drowse
            somewhere in
            California
feeling
the pressure
at my belt
my children
older
            my what
            is the right
            word
            my wife

blurring
in my mind
the past
even then
there
there were meals
there always
the simple measure
of growing

vegetables
here I
pick
at my broccoli
      my five year
      old ringing, drifting
      pushing toward me no
      blockery for me he yelled
      no blockery no no my three
      year old quietly: I
      don't want no trees

in the sky
time
turns
as my knife
turns on
my plastic tray

before
the mind
turns
before all
sounds

except
Rachmaninoff
throbbing
inside
my throbbing
head
        am I going
        or coming

ahead
the past

    and time before
    my wife
    my
    wife

California Poppies, Lilies of the Valley

turning from the wrong
dream turning
over the wrong-
ness

in my mind
you lay perfect-
ly still moving
        slightly

under all
of him turning
you inside
out of my
        reach

magnify-
ing you I
shrank before
        my-

self
turning to your
           back
then I saw
those california
road
poppies blowing

down you plucked
one hold-
           ing
on for more
than one
           blooming

Chico, California,
Spring 1965
_____

after
the rain
    after
the earlier
rain

    and
water rose
to the front
step
        you said do
        something call
        the water
        department

things
got worse
and it
stopped
raining

for
        months
the blossoms
        on
the orange
tree
in the back
yard
showed

something
else
        you said I
        don't want to
        talk
        about heat
and
the absence
of
clouds

listening
to Miriam
Makeba
      you painted on
      the kitchen
      walls love
      tastes
      like strawberries
mixing
beeswax
in muffin tins
with color
dripping
en-
caustic
      Chinese horses
      bulls
      unicorns
I framed

                them all
words
carefully
then
                be a man you
                said
one day
you
                said we can't
                make
                it isn't anything
                to do
                with you

and me
standing
beside the alien
rice
paper trees
watching

each other
care-
fully work-
      ing
around
the yard
     bone
dry

Going
_____

floating in inner
tubes bumping the creek
bed down
stream passing

a whole day before
my flight

our oldest on her
own waving up
                        ahead
the great
oaks over
us the creek
bending vines
hanging

            our buttocks
bumping rapids
easing into deep
water each

holding another
son

doubled now
moving a-
part this
boy I touch
was born

     in con-
cord mass-
achusetts then

     the black
     o's double
     floating that
boy you
arm to you
now
born three

thousand miles
a-
      way
here
this park
this and that
life here
I

am you
are they
are
come
with me

      together
      again
      the black inner
      tubes

I asked you
said again
your face
falling
down your
crying
head I

can't
move
away

     drifting
we saw
our little
girl
     there
     floating

still
moving up
ahead

The Return

we have come
back mouth
to mouth

backing
up to face
            our genitals
            knowing
more than we
did (not
listening
to years breasts to belly
up corn flowers
turning)

we have come
back from the dark
wood calling
            you ran in your yellow
            bathing suit under
            the giant tent-
            acular oaks

facing each
other we were married
people going
easy
      (if
    there is ever a
    chance for me)
there in bidwell
park
          hollywood's first
          sherwood forest and last little
          john

waxen colors over
our heads under
our feet there by
the horseshoe
court

we said
       soft
things
          to bring you
          back
here under me
holding
          your buttocks
beneath me pushing slowly
deeper

coming to
our senses every
where

Sunderland:
March Between Snows,
the First Baseball

_____

out in the back
yard the one bare
spot soft the pine
needles soft our sneakers
moving across the dark

dry ground my four
year old son swinging
the red plastic
bat now and
then hitting

the big flame
orange
ball thud-
ding it past
me talking

to himself I
said what
did you say
                underhanding
it to him once

more chopping
it he said I'm
a wind power
dad and the big
ball jumped out

of reach sideways
I moved looking
at him standing
square the bat
cocked

his face
serious I said

yes you are again
and again before
the first flakes

fell   inside
the house we
watched the juncos
and the black
hooded

chickadees feed over
the now white
ground
      miniature
california

quail my five
year old in the living
room doing
a puzzle shouting
it's incredible

For Robert Kennedy
—Sunderland, June 8, 1968—

[1]

moving back
and forth between
my beans
and the day long
news

yellow
colors lean
toward the closeness
and the intermittent
rain:
                dandelions (my young
                    son calls the minor
                    ones cubs)

flowering wild
strawberries in our uncut
grass

the first
lemon lilies among the ground
grapes

traveling from the edge
of the woods
to the woods
itself

[II]

something is tearing
up my
garden
a small selection
of diggings into
the corn
strewn

strays.   the squash
hills thrown
open

tombs, the white
sides of
    seeds scattered
like car doors

a few butter
beans just bare-
ly through
knocked over
         periscopes

Junkins' vegetable
junkyard

[III]

not everything
succumbed
to the paw-
    ing

42

young asparagus
pickerels
up among the ordinary
weeds
green antennae
grounded

in my own
garden
the grief
is just
as deep

Somewhere on Madaket Shore, the Anniversary of our Reconciliation

the fog horns
in the damp
air moving doors
          over
these dunes blowing
from the ocean full
          of certain
parts

of speech crashing
a little
way beyond
     the both of
us the whiteness
out

          there
across the sound
bringing

our bodies again
and again old shells
beach
grass rose
hips somewhere

     nearby
you are sketching bay
bushes
in the hooded terrycloth
robe we found
in the drawer
     of that big
house

quiet-
     ly darkening in
the spaces

Walking in the Fog
from the Wharf in
Nantucket With My
Four Year Old Son,
Each Carrying a
Three Pound Live
Lobster

———————————————

do they turn
            all
red
in the pot dad he
said the boat gone
in the fog behind
us our in-
laws moving

across the sound
muffled the new
transients
            passing
by look they have
lobsters bill one

said why
do

they have antennas
dad he said we don't
have antennas
                    passing
the remains
of a wedding on fair
street the paper
lays

sprinkled
at our feet a
            woman
turning
from her son angry
down the street hearing
the moving fog
horns

in the harbor
and beyond
the noises two
years ago we
left
    you at the dock
whispering

I'll see
you
    at the san
francisco air-
port
    now

on this
street hearing
again the horn
the boat always
        moving

toward
our houses passing

a lovely
blonde
        curled
on a doorstep
                saying
softly
oh screech

Poaching Blue-eyed Scallops
at Lake Coskata, Nantucket

here we are calmly
wading after
eight years
         the four of us four
         children later
         wading
bending all eight
of us picking
         knee
deep the water
rising these lovely
hinges twenty sapphires
apiece
     retinas
attached we fill
the floating bucket
     exclaiming
over each
one

        occasionally
        clacking in our palms false
        teeth

that party eight
years ago on the main-
land the four
of us
        (children)
jockeying through
the night passing
out-
        side the same
ocean crashing

remarkably
apart
        from our lives crashing
always within
earshot
we do not speak
of it

now the calm
tide coming in and out
there the waves crashing
the summer sun

going

    we finish collecting
our children growing
cold we wrap sweatshirts
             over them
riding the fenders past
        the samphire past
        the bayberry
and the beach
plums over
and over the sand
thinking of eight
years moving in

the dark
toward wauwinet

Opening Day of
Pheasant Season, 1968

---

noontime
I walked into the kitchen
a woodcock in each
pocket

      you got *two woodcocks* you
      said

standing by the sink
holding the long
beaks
the children exclaiming
my

      four year old poking
      down a lid forcing
      a wink (shouting
he SAW me dad)

ruffing the back
feathers our eyes
met remembering
that time before
my father
died leaving great east
lake stopping
the car in the alders near
the spring

        a mother wood-
cock leading four
chicks across
the road quietly

touching me making
me a sandwich you
spoke of a letter in the morning
mail we knew
had nothing to do

with wondrous brown
birds
bursting twenty feet into the air stopping

hovering

in flight that one
lonely
second before
whistling sideways

across the mind's
eye into the future
and beyond

the early Amherst
sky

A Spring Conversation:
the Passing of Words

huddling
together spinning jackstones
the children on the oak
floor
     our five year
     old yelling
ballerinas!
     catching the red
ball his face
flushed the fireplace
roaring pines

outside
green in the melting
snow   fingers
danc-
ing you edge a little
closer

The First Saturday
in Spring: Breakfast
at the Deerfield Inn

_____

this corner table
you said this
window
remember last
year the rain darkening
room the only couple

   here drinking
coffee eating eggs
our spun gold
ring
     there
on your hand
five blue
  and white stones rain
  crowding
the small spaces leaving

the house behind
our faded stucco
        mushroom squatting
in the helpless snow
(the babysitter bleary-
eyed our children poised
looking
east through television)

and we are
here again reaching across
the small
talk the spring sun
                table
cloth antique silver-
ware coffee English
muffins

reaching
        in the quiet

Mohawk town near
death feeling the smudged
Globe on our fingers smelling
the valley flowering across
the room

flowering
across the ever-
lasting Indian
war in Asia
the *Times* before.

us speaking across
our late and early
thirties
    consoling
each other's winter
comfort-
ing each other's
    spring

Steamed Clams on Pond Island,
the Quiet Drifting After

the cove settling
down the four o'clock wind

we gather our things,
row to the sloop
and haul anchor.

ghosting bayward the children turtlenecking
over the water star-
board the sea pale green
and the boulders lowering away,
fathoming from us, still

we started
the motor thought, puttered
hard thoughts
and spaces, petering
out at last the sun went
spinning, the boys jigging
two mackerel at the end of summer

it was all out there in the boat
drifting, quarreling off course
and on, eating bread by twilight
and my son Theodore asking is the top
of the sky as high as the bottom
                        of the sea—

the scaffold silhouette of the buoy
bonging, moping over
the tide, the tide
seven of us drifting on the dew point
of the season

it was at last the end
darkening
two families drifting in a Friendship
sloop in Blue Hill Bay

logged in
the summer gone

when they picked us up
we almost stayed to slip
by the red nun,
the black can,
the blacker cannery

but cruising in we drank beer
the children calling
from below
           there are TWO
bathrooms
and in the glaring docklights shook
hands and said goodnight